Praise for *dead boy*

Jason Morphew presents a supercharged, sometimes unsettling view of domestic life in *dead boy* (Spuyten Duyvil), his striking debut. While many of the situations described here seem familiar—a trip to CVS, a young daughter who explodes when told it's time for dinner—they're presented with an edginess and sharp intelligence that makes the poems pop. An underlying tension throughout the work stems from the death of Morphew's younger brother, whose absence is a constant presence... . [Morphew] easily moves through a range of emotions and settings. His perspective is always surprising.

— ELIZABETH LUND, THE WASHINGTON POST

In this startling debut collection, Jason Morphew creates a world more real than the reality we think we live—his poems evoke landscapes and innerscapes at once recognizable and surreal, sensual and death-haunted. ... The quest to live without numbing oneself (through narcotics or love or sex or material accommodations) is a struggle at the heart of these saturated, vividly intelligent and often wryly funny poems. This powerful book of poems will accompany you into your best days and your mislaid days, capturing exquisitely that odd realization of adulthood: "What now? Am I really mortal?"

— MEGHAN O'ROURKE, AUTHOR OF *SUN IN DAYS* AND *THE LONG GOODBYE*

I marvel at Morphew's ability to plumb the domestic for its latent existential horrors, its disturbing hilarity, the coolly controlled hysteria that is everywhere in the mundane, from blenders full of placenta to testicles bursting with the unexpected power of future-making. *dead boy* manages to be breezy, salty, sordid and downright serious all at once, newly mythologizing stories of love, death, and procreation few are lucky enough to glimpse in the brief spasm of living between the kept appointments and broken appliances that make up our lives.

— LEXA HILLYER, AUTHOR OF *ACQUAINTED WITH THE COLD*

Morphew is an iconoclast ... and, often, brilliant.

— ALEX M. FRANKEL, *THE ANTIOCH REVIEW*

This book almost convinced me to kill myself. A great stocking stuffer!

— JULIUS SHARPE, CREATOR OF *MAKING HISTORY*

EJECT CITY

Also by Jason Morphew

dead boy
Brooklyn, New York: Spuyten Duyvil Publishing, 2018

What to deflect when you're deflecting
Hoboken, New Jersey: Poets Wear Prada, 2017

In Order to Commit Suicide
n.p.: Floating Wolf Quarterly, 2012

EJECT CITY

POEMS BY
JASON MORPHEW

POETS WEAR PRADA • Hoboken, New Jersey

Eject City

Copyright © 2025 Jason Morphew

All rights reserved. Except for use in any review or for educational purposes, the reproduction or utilization of this work in whole or in part in any form by electronic, mechanical or other means, now known or hereafter invented, including xerography, photocopying and recording, or in any informational or retrieval system, is forbidden without the written permission of the publisher:

Poets Wear Prada
533 Bloomfield Street, Second Floor
Hoboken, New Jersey 07030
http://pwpbooks.blogspot.com

First North American Publication 2025
First Mass Market Paperback Edition 2025

Grateful acknowledgment is made to the following publications where some of these poems have appeared:

Confrontation Magazine, The Decadent Review, Lana Turner, Natural Bridge, Poetry Super Highway, Rat's Ass Review, Seneca Review, Sinking City Literary Magazine, Sip Cup, Smartish Pace, Yes Poetry, and *Twyckenham Notes.*

Publisher's Cataloging-in-Publication Data

Names: Morphew, Jason, 1972–, author.
Title: Eject City / poems by Jason Morphew.
Description: Hoboken, NJ: Poets Wear Prada, 2025.
Identifiers: LCCN: 2025934570 | ISBN: 9781946116291
Subjects: LCSH Morphew, Jason. | Poetry, American — 21st century. | BISAC BIOGRAPHY & AUTOBIOGRAPHY / Memoirs | POETRY / Subjects & Themes / Death, Grief, Loss | POETRY / Subjects & Themes / Family | POETRY / Subjects & Themes / Love & Erotica | POETRY / Subjects & Themes / Places
Classification: LCC PS3613. O755255 E5 2025 | DDC 811.6—dc23

Printed in the U.S.A.

Front Cover Image: Mark Baum (1903 – 1997), *Both Sides of the Argument*, 1984, acrylic on canvas, 56 x 72 inches
Author Photo: Matilda Morphew, 2024

For
Gary Joe Morphew
1953 – 2018

"... this even-handed justice
Commends the ingredients of our poison'd chalice
To our own lips."

—William Shakespeare, *Macbeth*, Act 1, Scene 7

Table of Contents

Touch Anywhere to Get Started	3
Visitation	4
Press Release: Confederate Sculpture Garden	5
Little moments when you're married	6
We listen to another's pain	7
Gene Watson	8
There's no way to love me	9
When there was a music industry	10
Ikey	11
Sargassum	12
Unforgiven	13
Formaldehyde	14
Unconditional Love	15
It's Very Simple	16
I am the destroyer	17
Now that my father's ash	18
When I Knew You Are a Poet	19
I love you time	20
Murder Rap	21
Suzanne	23
Suzanne II	24
Mattress Store as Cemetery	25
Men's Warehouse	26
Bell's Palsy	28
Milo #2	29
I sleep next to pool equipment	30
Jerry Jones	31
Where is all the fun hidden?	32
Hoax	33
Classical music	34

Crying when suicidal	*35*
The Paris Review	*36*
Snow White Cafe	*37*
male dancers	*39*
Sorry for My Resurrection	*40*
Lyric	*41*
Gregory/Orr	*42*
Floyd Davies	*43*
Unemployment	*45*
Often on Wednesday nights	*46*
Teddy Boy	*47*
Divorce	*48*
Lunch Poem	*49*
Tyranny	*50*
Heritage	*51*
Politics	*52*
Naramore Sonata #1 in T-Minor	*53*
unspoken	*54*
San Clemente	*55*
Party of One	*56*
Massage Gun	*57*
120 Grand Bar	*59*
Stepwidowmaker	*60*
Brakes	*61*
Women v. Robots	*63*
Me Too	*64*
Biathanatos	*65*
Slow Burn	*67*
Fucking in Teatro La Fenice	*69*
This is where I'll go back	*70*
Hope for the Future	*71*
Haiku for the Duration	*72*

Acknowledgments	*73*
About the Author	*74*
About the Artist	*75*

EJECT CITY

Touch Anywhere to Get Started

but when it's over
be music
I'll never know
you almost stole
from chambers
near my imagination
curved bodies
with vibrating holes
rhyming me
unready for you.

Visitation

For one hour my father will exist

in a state of visitation

reached by racist

atoms in lapels

urning fragments of forty

carbon faces lining prefab walls

like confused cancer cells.

Keith Richards smoked his father

mine smoked me

these are my ashes

spread me like the space

between religious sounds.

Press Release: Confederate Sculpture Garden

Last night we put them on the moon
in frozen snowflake form
fanning from American flag
bleached white by the sun.

Their details disappear.
Choiring them here
gave them awful power
as if on the march again
in titan scope dropping
into passing trees
a certain length of rope

space the only means
of muffling the scream
their proximity creates
the scream whose phantom
memory the slackjaw
ceaselessly fellates.

Kneel Nazis
find your knees borrow
telescopes and pray
while the inward wonder
if this is how the gods
always go away.

Little moments when you're married

for a discount
on dry cleaning
in the 90s
on the Lower East Side
and your Polish wife's
name ends with -*ska*
so you say to the gaunt
gray Polish cleaners
you're *Jason Kochanska*
they blink in Polish
through deep glasses
and concede your
tiny tapered pants
which you flutter home
to her apartment
where you should be
paying rent you say
what arose she
laughs she thought
you knew men's names
end with -*ski* in Poland
and your friend her
roommate who
introduced you to her
needs you
to be a man
so you get your own apartment
which leads to your divorce
from them
and New York City
henceforth you travel everywhere
on skis of manhood
painted like penises
pants still tapered
ever more deathsome
and afraid.

We listen to another's pain

as if it were a different species
contaminating ours
virus from another world

when pain is the world
we are the disease
weakening our host.

Gene Watson

Often sitting at the bar
at El Compadre on Sunset Blvd
eyebanging the abyss
I imagine I am Gene Watson
on the cover of his album
*Should I Come Home (Or
Should I Go Crazy)?*
I try not to write poems
about country music
because the poetry demographic
and my children's need for food
yet here we are here I am
going crazy having just taught
the *Metamorphoses* then
Pinocchio stabbing in
between with a corkscrew
my left hand which my father
forced me to throw from
as a righthanded child
because he wanted me to be
Sandy Koufax and couldn't
see his antisemitism.
I still can't throw from my right hand
and am raising Jews
with my father's last name.
Mobile home is mobile
vengeance I'm almost
always there.

There's no way to love me

you shrieked
at five years old
having reached already
the end of language
the lightless path
where I wait
always for you.

When there was a music industry

and everyone was air
I thanked the mobile notary
for echo and the glare
in my warehouse always snowing
in my roofless Wrangler going
to parties shows and showers
my heart had artificial powers
I plugged it in
I wasn't there
on linen couches
knocking Clarks with fame
I didn't have a name
I was air
warm beneath a single check
in Spaceland liking Beck
less than the industry assumed
I was air I was groomed
I wasn't dapper I was doomed
to become a man
but I remember being air
and the music of me there.

Ikey
1974 – 2014

Always in a hundred bands
late for all rehearsals

still not on our England tour
or in the concert on the mountain

not in the Knitting Factory
on 9/11 or shorts of Razorback

in elfin drummer's bed
no damage left for ecstasy

or failed successful music
always in a hundred bands

late for all rehearsals

still.

Sargassum

Passive dinosaur apocalypse
    on banks of Yucatán —
                Señor Whore apocalypse
                    ATM bombing azure flan
                        after art and science mastering
                            the sarcastic orgasm
                        waves of ironic joy
                become Darwin's disembodied beard
            strangling your children
         too many nutrients
      for their deforested intestines
their late hearts beating
        like water bottles
    contracting
            expanding
                      into profitsharing biospheres
where the dirtyminded diver
delves —
    how   do   robots   party
          how will the robots kill themselves?

Unforgiven

Revenge
can't be had
on the past

is the devil's
and my dilemma
the future's never

near the past
is always here
if you believe in life

and education
come culture
meet me tonight

in nightmares
I'll fuck your wife
you'll take my children

where words
and weaning
imperfectly remembered

blur the air
into meaning
fire on a baby

father's baby
daughter's fingers
bestowing blindness

on milked Milton's
pseudonymous
synth pop dawn.

Formaldehyde

On the Caddo River
there's a train trestle
and a swimming hole
down a dirt path
from a cemetery
where my brother
and his recent ancestors
bleed formaldehyde
into the water table.
It's good for you
and children
diving from the trestle
into chemicals below
it keeps you dead
and white longer
skincare for the departed
poison for the getting
ready to go.

Unconditional Love

My father's siblings
when he died
texted that his wife
gave him what I didn't:
unconditional love.
This surprised me
never having known
conditional love.
If there are conditions
it's family
sports religion
barring a father's
only child from his only
father's funeral.
It's a cynical poem
groveling in rags
of language
for a kiss of blood.

It's Very Simple

You grab an axe
and take your family
downstairs
to the basement
you place a wooden block
before them raise the axe
above your head
wince and split the wood
saying *Satan*
is trying to destroy us!
No matter what occurs
your wife your kids
and your stepdemon
saw you briefly
meaning business.

I am the destroyer

of webs I carry a magic
orange stick that lengthens like
a plastic man in my hands
I give death an erection
while my children watch
me endorse murder
father scattered
mother muzzled
I swing my stick and kill
imagining my own web
will not be destroyed
I will be loved forever
inching my unknown wall.

Now that my father's ash

around me
as he always was
a shifting robe
of darkness too rich
for secondhand
too poor for
merely breathing
without sufficient
magic for vanishing
together he couldn't
teach me how
to do it but being
a family doctor now
I'm invisible forever
behind a velvet
smoking jacket
a modest bong
curtain habit
and a leaping boy
with lungs
he never entered.

When I Knew You Are a Poet

Late as always
breath as dragons
on a January 8 am
  diving the
    narrow
   mile
    down
to Wonderland
you were 5
and stopped
to sit on a
neighbor's steps
to remove a rock
from your shoe
and scratch your foot
so leisurely your sister
the man who owned
the steps and I all stared
in admiration but that's
not the poetry
I mean that moments
later rounding
hedges by the house
where we returned
the dog that bit you
your soft hands spread
and you exclaimed
Guys guys wait
now I have a SOCK
in my shoe!
which we varied
endlessly
until unto the mortal
world of others
I relinquished you.

I love you time

for your wretched arms
around me
laurel chains
iron wreaths
surround me
at night I call you
strangling but in the day
you're breathing
my children grow
poems flow
everything is leaving
love is grief
death is the final stage
of grieving.

Murder Rap

Every parent knows
blood stains shit doesn't
you can run and ask my
pop star first cousin
by pop I mean fly
by fly I mean hit
made it to the minors
then his left knee quit
went to Purdue to learn horticulture
money was roadkill, he was a vulture
really got rich selling deer semen
how he got it out
I leave to your bedroom dreamin
now let me admit, I didn't come to flirt
I made myself a Morphew google alert
so I could see when my exstepmother dies
so I can correct her obituary lies
that may sound dark but I'm about to get darker
into my inbox space spun a parallel parker
a message that blocked me into my mind
my former idol Barry was suspected of crime
on Mother's Day his wife Suzanne went missin
the last time I saw her she was witnessin
to me about becoming a born again Xian
which I became . . . when I was 6
now I was 41, there's no comprehending these hicks
I started watching Colorado news day and night
my face lit by YouTube light
my family's history explored by freaks
I started wondering: are they coming for me?
Am I guilty? Did I kill Suzanne?
I rejected my family to become a man
which feels like a form of murder
poisoning pigeons
when you're supposed to be a birder
the climax came one afternoon
I was editing a novel in my favorite room

the cis man cave where we have a big screen
where a male stripper named Chocolaté's been seen
the FBI was tearing up a work site like paper
where Barry had worked as the lone landscaper
the live stream feed fed me greed
for more information I had an infantile need
the breathless host of a true crime show
said she'd just received a text from somebody who knows
Barry's been arrested, the body's been found
under a slab of concrete that my boy laid down
my wife and I started rehearsing the speech
we'd make to our kids about infamy's reach
but wait hold up the Sheriff steps to the mic
he'd already made it clear
my cousin's not someone he likes
he says no body's been recovered
no one's incarcerated
since that shock I've more casually awaited
word that somehow Suzanne got free
became a dead again Xian somewhat like me
maybe she's safe in a darkened place
early film noirs flickering on her face . . .
Barry's back in his alpine palace
sippin deer sperm from an antler chalice
I'm all the way west with the same last name
standing on the shore with my back to pain
to reinvent yourself to a small degree
requires every ounce of your energy
Is it worth the trouble? How would I know?
watched *Hamilton* last night
it gave me this flow.

Suzanne

What would you find in my femur
marrow—straight and narrow
Xanax crystals of
palindromic cross
funny footnotes from *Harper's Magazine*
fused with Freixenet and colchicine
residue of revenue
love and shame and joy
brittle shards of credit cards
marriages miscarriages
a sound past questions
brown light breaking free?

Suzanne II

Deep time suggests
our lives don't happen
not even long enough
to streak the stone
nothing could be more poetic
than centuries wasted
saying what we are
Michelangelo's chisel
Freud's glasses
perimortem trauma
is an injury
around the time of death
without evidence
of healing
who can say what happens
how high the hematoma
how deep the angel's
condescension inside
the birth canal?

Mattress Store as Cemetery

       I wanted to fuck
       not   only
         everything
       through   you
       but   also
         nothing
    in us a billion
    rectangular beds

Men's Warehouse
after James Dickey

Here they are
the blank eyes
open if they have
worked in a cubicle
it's a cubicle if in
construction it's
steel toes and
4x4 forever.
Having no souls
they have come
anyway despite
their knowing
weakness battens
and they rise.
The blank eyes open.
To match them
the cold floor
flowers outdoing
what is required—
the beigest wall
the sharpest nail.
It could not be a place
of men without blood
so they hunt
callscript and hammer
more perfect
than they can believe
they stalk more loudly
crouch on couches
and their descent
upon the soft ears
of their prey takes
centuries a coffin
floating through
waterfalls of joy

and the hunted
know this
as their life to
strut under
high windows
iPhone gazing
in full knowledge
of the glory
above them
and to feel
no fear
but acceptance
compliance
fulfilled without
pain at the soft
skull's center
they tremble
they strut under
the window
they fall
they are torn
they rise
they bleed again.

Bell's

When I'm depressed
because I can't not
joke with each other.
Its link to intelligence
Intelligence is a mental illness.
If I say I'm dumb I hate myself.
there was a pill to make
Few cheeks worth rhyming
like payday loan interest
foreclosing laughs later I revised
over darkened tennis
everything we know
a caterer in clogs
while Slash and Duff
the only good ones
half herpe
half devotion half

Palsy

I watch cable news
smile when two hosts
Depression is a mental illness.
has been proved.
If I say I'm smart I'm arrogant.
Bud Hyde said he wished
me love myself.
with sheets compound
dreams authorities advised
on a mountain under a demi lune
all the imagery of every poem
merely bifurcation
forking your gummied wife
serenade your absent children
ever written
half autism
division.

Milo #2

Spatial relationships
dimly recalled
generate time—
my 6 yr old
still counting the dog
that died when she was 4
as the 3rd oldest member of our family
that space unfilled
in air around her
the forgiving tail unclutched
where did she come from?
We say we conceived her
in the Galapagos on the *Cachalote*
surrounded by couples from Canada and Spain
one whose clothes all bore a dog's paw logo
but life a dream
maybe she made us
out of Milo maybe we're a bark
in a dream he's having in heaven
about Matilda
and the space we see
the time we feel
all imaginary
don't foretell dispersal
but crush us further
into congregation
our language nothing
but a home protecting sound.

I sleep next to pool equipment

window walls without curtains
and every time the pool man comes
I'm either jacking off or dozing.
Perhaps you think always I
am either jacking off or dozing.
How would I be writing this?
No he and I are married
to pleasure's damp oblivion
never guessing I'm forgiven
I jerk boxers over ass
and roll from bed
as if under fire
the hill a bomb above us
or I've just finished
flaming and the tiny little leaves
he gathers in his elfin cap
are pieces of disease
that dream me while I nap.

Jerry Jones

pissed all over my bathroom
which I interpreted as a
power play like
*Fuck you I'll piss all over
your bathroom* then
he approached me
at Nobu in Malibu
Johnny Walker Blue
in trembling hand
and said *Jason it
wasn't a power play
I'm just an old man*
which I guess is why
he stole the show
I developed for him
the world's a toilet
he does the best he can.

Where is all the fun hidden?

my daughter asks my wife
in the Perot Museum of Nature and Science
cartoon hydrocarbons giggling in the walls
Step-Mashed Potatoes
with a perm for gravy

failed suicide Owen Wilson
narrating the Big Bang
Dave Berman's big success
underway
dudes from Big D
going bigger
according to neutral angles
of their nature

AWAKE

with your fanny pack
rapture Xians
and low church Jews never naked

doggy your wife
on the giant plastic
fracking drill

the world a racist diorama
we're quaking corporately inside.

Hoax

There's a big dispute
about what's happening
in my heart—
is it manmade
and why isn't anyone
offended by the question?
Experts in corruption
say no one measured
my heart before
I got children
so who's to prove
what makes what
let's give him another horror
and they have a suicidal
point which given
what goes for normal
makes perfect sense.
No need to get all living
let's just agree it's changing
its pressures rise floods
of blood are coming
tennis may be too late
but on further planets
if my children make it
after the attack
I hope they hear this
humming in the void
turn to their kids
and say *Imagine
if he hadn't tried.*

Classical music

worries me
especially
Beethoven
when the
Budapest
String
Quartet
gets its
catgut
interwoven
I calm
myself by
thinking *This
is a record
they released
surely no one
dies* but
research reveals
they're all
deceased
which confirms
my best
suspicions.

Crying when suicidal

is like coughing
when choking
speaking
when feeling
fucking in love—
essence
abandoned
survival
decomposed

The Paris Review

All my lies
are four hours long
in a refrigerator
next to a telephone
that only dials
1-800 commercials
for rockabilly boxes.
All my lies
are untucked polos
on evangelical pastors.
All of them
are Trey Owen's fingers
in Allison Robert.
None of them are sexual.
Sex is God's body
moving in our lives
tricking us into
fucking each other.
We're all fucking God
His bunny ears
behind us
in the desert I rode my motorcycle
past a pet grooming store
called *Doggy Style*
extra gas can
barfing in my ass
karma for being kareful
my brand
anxiety my skin
a lie of fire.

Snow White Cafe

is a bar
in Hollywood
where I ate lunch
and read every day
because it was always
empty the bartender
played Depeche Mode
and bought every
third beer.
It had a large screen
I never saw anything on
until my dad came to visit
during football season.
The Razorbacks were playing
Alabama or an idea like that
and my dad stared stars
through players' legs
as Depeche delivered
Cokes and lagers.
The game was tight
and late like a drunk
plumber and my dad
extravagantly corn syrupped
was making animal
noises and leaping from
his chair as the plays
departed. Depeche and I
locked eyes I telepathed
all was well all was
groovy this was my father
not an addict I'd collected
at the Army Navy
Surplus Store. The game
entered the afterlife
Depeche didn't
like it further tourists

were confused
by Dad juxtaposed
with Doc
and Happy
no perspective
sporting
on the walls.
It's almost over
I think I said and
I'm ready for another.
That's when the last play
effloresced the last vector
for victory just as Depeche
arrived my father
uppercut the air and
vertically exploded
a missile out of misery
something dying
you feel privileged
to be frightened by.
Did beer go gliding?
Did Razorbacks win a game?
Did I ever return?
Who could say blinded
by a passion
I must live as love.

male dancers

how could it possibly be
ascertained from whence
they rise
fatherless energies
twirling packages
of lies

Sorry for My Resurrection

It really hurt my stepfather
when I fell asleep
while hunting
and he had to let a turkey live
because it was near my body
covered in leaves
hands folded
lying on my back
what the turkey
and my motherfucker didn't know
was they were at my funeral
and their disappointment
wasn't that I wasn't theirs
for eating or to eat them
but that I was only briefly dead
unshot jerkoff Jesus
soon again would greet them.

Lyric

Trying to remember
the last idea
I bring you this
lesser child
of music this
violent bygone
trend.

Gregory/Orr

I can't get the Poetry Foundation
to post my biography
on a sufficiently shameful tree
the elegant elm against which
my brother exploded his face
fifteen years ago last week.
That's the kind of sentence
lover blurbers call *surreal*.
All you horrible babies
in bed by beautiful books
eating pussy—take note.
They blurb you.
They push their brothers
to their deaths. They make
brothers who push sisters
from top bunks onto
hardwood floors.
They vomit and stare.
What do you have to say?
What do you have to hear?
Are you?

Floyd Davies

Blake and me of course
smashed in Plato's cave
(JR's Lightbulb Ballroom, Arkansas Ozarks)
when he challenged an Irish bartender
to fight the following day
saying "Shamrock" could find Blake by the name
Floyd Davies—

such courage
doesn't find its way
onto Olympic broadcasts
which is my complaint
about the Mainstream Media

I've always wondered why
that name what drunken synapse
kinked those sounds together
hicked exotic
forehandle from another era
Shamrock's acceptance demonstrates
a Floydlike daring
not to fight

not to kill not to be jailed
not to be known
not to have feelings
not to be Blake or Jason
not to be drunk not to be lost
not to be alive and open

years later my father died
after not speaking to me again
for years or knowing his grandchildren
and a twisted strap his wife
obituarized him by naming
herself his lone survivor

and onto the Condolences Page
beneath my father's name
on the website of Ruebel Funeral Home
came a comment from Floyd Davies
why he cared a son remains
can only be conjectured
maybe he was caroused encaved
compelled again to go

Unemployment

In the hot tub reading journals
Joan Armatrading in the rocks
wishing I loved poetry and music
or anything
basketball and travel
some people really love to read
on Mulholland on my motorcycle
I don't love movement
or even leaning into death
it's the minimum I accept
stranded always in the foothills
of my greed wanting to learn
mountain climbing despite
despising mountains
and climbing
all those ropes to untangle
no vocation worth my love
eternally unflung
from cliffs
at anything.

Often on Wednesday nights

at Second Baptist Church
in Hot Springs
when there was a music industry
hairspray from a slightly
larger hole would appear
and present a film
proving every rock star
worshipped Satan.
All those albums
Prince Ozzy Judas Priest
at home awaited
my soft canals
so shamefully
I was persuaded
to discard them atop
our oblique driveway
courageously including
the first Pogues album
because evangelicals
cannot perceive
skepticism as faith—
nevermind this
is about Prince
lifelong Xian
black and sexual
when nice people smirk
at my mystic rage
I think of those authorities
fiends around me
pale and gray
and my mother's words
after the trashmen
washed my LPs away—
I'm proud of you son
death metal deep
echoing forever
on hell's PA.

Teddy Boy

My 4 yr old has a cis male gendered doll
blond and cis like him that he calls his son.
In bed before I leave he holds out the doll
and says *Kiss your grandson goodnight.*
I'm 45 and may never know another grandchild
but this feel of felt and yarn.
I think my son knows that
love is running toward a precipice
you didn't know was there.

Divorce

Pushing an empty stroller
down Santa Monica Blvd
as the gay bars open
acting casual so as not
to seem insane yet
knowing the grieving
need to speak to its
vacancy to bend down
and embrace life
on the other side
of contiguous love
drowned pounded
and surrounded
by the future not
having him with me.

Lunch Poem

The bartender at Trunks
in WeHo gave me
a margarita removed
his shirt and ordered
a burrito on
his phone telling
the man next to me
I didn't know it was that simple.
How could he know
I'm an artless symbol
that the air and I
are sequels
since my coauthor
tapped himself
like ash into a tray?

Tyranny

My daughter cheating
on a poster where
you find hidden objects
and put stickers on them
turning it over
to see the answers
I say *Stop*
it's not fun without the mystery
she does it anyway
proud when the images
are exhausted.

Heritage

Driving home from the airport
from sustained turbulence
white knuckling Seneca
from Arkansas where I was barred
from my father's funeral
by halfeyed vipers in Russell sweats
pill bottle of ashes
labeled *Dear Old Dad*
bouncing behind me with the toothpaste
my daughter asked me how
many cigarettes my father smoked
in what for brevity's sake we'll unlaughingly proclaim
his life.
Let's see—two packs of Reds a day
for fifty years?
Maybe around 700,000.
Dad you don't have a Daddy
now you only have a Mommy
to take care of you.
Yes honey and the person
Philip Morris who recently
expanded into electronic
he's my new daddy
you see dear the world is nothing
but step relatives
biology is bigotry
love's ready for the future now.

Politics

Born white
evangelical scum
I whacked away
my rural life
to forget
my failure
as sperm—
now I drive
my canyon life
into my lyric
Jewish wife
to forget
my failure
as sperm—
but it never comes
despite recycled mountains
centuries onscreen
the Alzheimer Maneuver
Ricky Reaper's redneck reach
around for refugees
righteous ready
ashy and obscene.

Naramore Sonata #1 in T-Minor

There's a cello in this poem
sawing soft lit scenery
forcing units of the self
through narrow corridors
where families form
leaving dummy heads behind
having sex with hypothermia
riding power cords
through midnight tides
of Xmas correspondence
escape the only art
when the medium is life
see now the moon at tee ball
seemless and unliving
be now the cello's bow
frying all that it can be
the flaming infant son
of a Garland County Circuit Judge
act now and get half free.

unspoken

sometimes
vaguely

how vast

San Clemente

Photographs admit
I can't acknowledge
this you're so
beautiful to stay
would be remiss
so I enter another
death the nine
millionth one
today a cloud
the only proof I stood
and watched you play.

Party of One

All I'd eaten was sand
and salad when I moderated
the Q&A after the premiere
of the Shakespeare movie
at the Nuart on Santa Monica
but I'd had cocktails
in the bath
book in hand
alive
to possibility
and the awkward result
built a window
on my being which
was not my job
it never is
I freely volunteer.

Massage Gun

Tautologically
in a place
where every phrase
sounds like
a poem title
left hamstring
tight to
snapping
hot tub
loud and useless
I'm on the hunt
for relief
from a gun
that shoots
your muscles.
Ed Hirsch
might end
the poem there
from what
I'm reading
lately maybe
he can do
the splits
and doesn't
care or need
to stretch
innately
but Hyperice
has a piece
known on the
street as Hypervolt
for merely
all your plastic
your pain can
commit suicide
and you can do
gymnastics

the class war
is a lazy one
it doesn't merit
capitalization
its weapons
are the soul
reliable narration.

120 Grand Bar

It takes a lot of flannel
to survive the 80s
in your mind
all those neglected women
in padded pews
rewinding repressed
cassettes on your penis's PA
as thirty church choked
miles away halfbabies crash
coupes into piñatas like
dawn adulterating dew
it's not like she married
a bank president
or that their pond
is named for you.

Stepwidowmaker

All this music
going to waste
the western wardrobe
of my excyborg's heart
dawn glory
filling Sandpa's atrium
like an LED
crucifixion

Come in

a good chambermaid
weeps
not of the unavoidable
eviction

did you think spiders climb
they fly
from Bellaire Dr
to Mt Sequoyah
threading skin
you thought was sky
to sentimental
paranoia.

Brakes

The joke
is not a joke
the joke is life
me and my 5 yr old
boy at different corners
of an empty table
in a sushi restaurant
so he can sit next
to his imminent mother
whom he *just likes
better* than me.
When I was 5
my mother married
again and my father
in fury slammed
his brakes
on the freeway
to scream
he was my only dad.
As a richer man raised me
my father floored it
marrying an adopted woman
divorced with abandoned daughters
and said he was their dad.
It was even in his obituary.
When I hitchhiked
truth into the local paper
the abysm woman
barred me from
my father's funeral.
O unceasing folly
O me of mighty faith
in Xlessness and nondivorce
midnight freeway music
crashes and uncrashes
are the same
something clear

will stain you
hereby hear my wise advice
valet what cannot be afforded
throw not a bill on Bill Knott's garbage
gaze not at gutterends
shaped like Arkansas
recall that Gore Vidal
could not absorb it all
tell your son
you never met
your grandfather
had a scar beneath
his bottom lip
from when his father drove
through rain into a train
while his son was softly sleeping
make him know
the graveyard tableau
of you at 3
scattering the scar
back onto his father
through transparent fish
read this and rise
say I was given to exaggeration
who fed me with mystical vibration
when I was starved with lies
say even now your father tries
to find a prayer
that makes him born again
this time not of men
never knowing where he was
honored to have been briefly
close to you
dying's what we do
when your project launches
thereof
seek help
to send out your senescence
in a glass as cold as love.

Women v. Robots

is how men
return let us
show you how we fight
our minds free
to see that we
are less than
little sticks to start a fire with
let us spend the conflagration
shielding you
with our disintegration
peace was always obsolete
but not assistance
those endowed
with beauty will
romance those endowed
with brilliance will write
grants turn us out
for organ harvests
under the autumn moon
the robots will seek feelings
offer them our doom
confuse them
with our bodies
blame us for God and money
when the robots organize a dance
send us a single phalanx
marching down the drive
we'll be ready
in dress shoes
to lose you
another night
alive.

Me Too

I want to live
in Fontaine de Vaucluse
where the Sorgue outrageous
as opened vein
in writing wrists
of Petrarch and Casanova
makes death
pretentious
the last distracting dream
an obsolete heart
hides.

Biathanatos

Glow in the glass
of my closed
bedroom door
suggests fire
on the other side
though the night
is cold my breathing
like a glutton
feasting on a world
of suffering.
Where are the angels
when I dance
where are the police
when I make children?
Authority's cosmology
is corrupt and doesn't have
a message but my daughter
for Xmas asked for
all the powers
making several Santas frown
embarrassing grandparents
I tried to give them to her
via viable vial
emptied of mystic crystal chips
filled with tree green sugar water
which she drank and smiled
and sighed and said
I feel funny I feel different
since then she's essayed
supernatural acts
lifting me with her legs
starting out a ping pong master
counting seconds in the air
as flying slamming
the bowling ball
into the lane like Atlas
should with a world

that does not repay
its dreamers.

Slow Burn

The insult long unfolding
every envelope tinged with red
work vanished
from the curriculum vitae
bonged for brother in law
after the sixty threesome
replacing parking spaces
with Jacuzzis of clear glass
where children bathe in sewage
screenplay smart yet stupid
poem white and dead
article half unwritten
Oblomov half unread
abandoned by the controversies
too unfamous to offend
lectured by tv writers
at his birthday dinner
on the topic of his PhD
wife and children of a different god
color of house unidentifiable
in the glare of preschool pickup time
changing the joke about being half Italian
(from the waist down)
to the one about being half alive
waste up in the abysm's unremarkable archive
too old to hop a box
on the lonesome tenure track
too young for nothing
parent parties interrupting
the one already underway
the red spot on Jupiter
all the time every day
he turns to you in desperation—
weren't you his favorite band
didn't music radiate in basements
weren't women in the sheets
reading the Earl of Rochester

before cannabis was legal
and America was gone—
even his rebellion was obedient
his faithlessness an act of faith
in further money
fat again in the Vatican
twisted as Solomon's columns
whispering to halfsisters
There may not be a God
or an objective measure of success
but there is wealth and Amarone
and a penalty for hope
a number he's about to learn
he hides it from the children
during the tee ball games
he coaches how to feel
when accidentally not making errors
receive your glory like an Oxycontin dad
moaning in a psych ward *You've got the curse*
a gaslit Bible gave him life
and called it love a talking tree
might as well have maintained silence
lo the mystic thud of low church faith
which isn't faith when everyone you know
believes it what's real to him isn't real
to others there's a word for that
he builds beside his sleeping bride
listening to coyotes eating terriers
bouncing like a Slazenger between Agamben and PornHub
giving the empty dose pen another try
what makes it vibrate
when nothing's left inside?

Fucking in Teatro La Fenice

during Mozart's *Idomeneo*
once before and once after
intermission in our private box
not drunk enough
not to care as much as we
didn't wait when we saw
we were alone I always wonder
when I travel in my chains
where anybody fucks
where can everybody be
inside each other everywhere
when our scattered fathers
occupy us there.

This is where I'll go back

this life
these moments
my children fog
recurring in the hall
my children's hands
verging on me
strong and tortured

this is where I'll journey
to this thick luxury
of skin and music
my unearned authority
on the long elaborate failure
of the laziness of love
all this rich endlessness
of fear and pajamas

here is where I'll hover
covered in piss and kisses
when they're gone and
gorgeous and I have
nowhere else to go.

Hope for the Future

She calls me to the window
to see a flower on our new elm tree
and realizes as I arrive
that the flower is a hummingbird
on a branch so light
it's hardly upright
I tell her hummingbirds are spirits
of Aztec warriors and she says
That's Pap Paw
looking over us
even though he didn't die
in the war so absurd
there can be no question.

Haiku for the Duration

Yes it passes in
a flash but without the light
why would darkness be?

Acknowledgments

The author extends his thanks to the following publications where some of these poems first appeared.

Confrontation Magazine	"Hoax"
The Decadent Review	"Classical music"
Lana Turner	"I sleep next to pool equipment," "Sorry for My Resurrection," and "Politics"
Natural Bridge	"Now that my father's ash" and "Lunch Poem"
Poetry Super Highway	"Suzanne"
Rat's Ass Review	"Gene Watson"
Seneca Review, 50th Anniversary Edition	"Bell's Palsy," "Milo #2," "Jerry Jones," "The Paris Review," "Gregory/Orr," "Unemployment," and "Teddy Boy"
Sinking City Literary Magazine	"Formaldehyde"
Sip Cup	"Naramore Sonata #1 in T-Minor" and "Stepwidowmaker"
Smartish Pace	"When there was a music industry"
Twyckenham Notes	"Unconditional Love" and "Heritage"
Yes Poetry	"Men's Warehouse"

"When there was a music industry" was a finalist for *Smartish Pace*'s 19th Erskine J. Poetry Prize, judged by Stephen Reichert, in 2020.

"Ikey" appears in the liner notes to the author's live album *England Tour -9/03* (Unread Records, 2018).

About the Author

Jason Morphew started life in a mobile home in Pike County, Arkansas; a Yale graduate, he has a PhD in English Renaissance Literature from UCLA. *The Washington Post* reviewed his first full-length collection of poems, *dead boy*, on January 31, 2018, calling it one of the three "best poetry collections to read this month." As a singer-songwriter, once signed to Capitol and Sony/ATV, he's released 13 albums on the indie labels Brassland, Ba Da Bing, Max, and Unread. His song "Bring Your Sorrow Over Here" was featured in the cult classic film *Niagara, Niagara* (Director Bob Gosse, 1997). His writing appears in *The Daily Beast*, *Los Angeles Review of Books*, *Seneca Review*, *Bellevue Literary Review*, *Lana Turner*, *The Cortland Review*, and *Smartish Pace*, among other places. Morphew teaches English at Stanford Online High School and lives with the bestselling author Lauren Kate and their two children in Laurel Canyon.

About the Artist

Mark Baum (January 2, 1903 – February 8, 1997) was a renowned Polish American artist of the 20th century. He was best known for his cityscapes and landscapes. Notably, his figurative works are part of the permanent collections at the Metropolitan Museum of Art and the Whitney Museum of American Art. Later in life, Baum explored non-objective and spiritual themes, exemplified by the painting on the cover of this book. Two major exhibitions showcasing this later work were held posthumously: one at Oakland's Krowswork Gallery (2016) and another at the Michael Kohler Arts Center in Sheboygan, Wisconsin (2019).

A NOTE ON THE TYPE

Text for this book is set in Monotype Garamond, considered to be among the most legible typefaces for the printed page. Designed by Fritz Max Steltzer at Monotype Corporation, Garamond is named after the punch-cutter Claude Garamont (c. 1480 – 1561) but more closely follows the roman letter forms of a later punch cutter named Jean Jannon and the italic forms cut by Robert Granjon.

www.ingramcontent.com/pod-product-compliance
Lightning Source LLC
Chambersburg PA
CBHW020809160426
43192CB00006B/500